Editor's Note

Glorious Fashion Magazine communicates the character of God through faith-based subjects that promote spiritual growth and inner beauty. This winter issue features casual styles that are trendy as well as versatile just in case it snows. The black & denim ensemble I'm wearing was perfect for the cool weather while photographing The Grand Canyon and later that evening for dinner. In addition, you'll find a variety of topics that help you stay healthy, active and flawless all season long.

Editor in Chief
Gloria Humphrey

CONTENTS

The Dressing Room 5
Cultivating Inner Beauty

Poem 11
Winter Wonder

Fashion 12
Cool & Casual

Travel 15
Featured Destination:
Arizona

Six Health & Beauty Tips 30

Wedding Day Passion 42

The Grand Canyon

Glorious
FASHION MAGAZINE

THE DRESSING ROOM

Get
Changed!

REMOVE THE OLD GARMENT

......put off the old man with his deeds;
Colossians 3:9

Deeds: an action that is performed

intentionally or consciously;

ones character

The idea of the old garments or the sinful nature being removed gives notice to the fact that a new garment is presently available. Because our nature is sinful at the time of birth by way of one man's disobedience, we are invited or called (since the call creates obedience) to receive righteousness by the obedience of one man - The Man Jesus Christ! (Read Romans 5) Although many of us are invited to receive the free gift of salvation, we still must

choose to accept the grace it provides, which gives us the power to change. In this way we remove the old garment by exchanging the evil deeds of the flesh (Galatians 5:19-21) and their power over us for the fruit of the spirit (Galatians 5:22-24)

"I will greatly rejoice in the LORD, my soul shall be joyful in my God; for he hath clothed me with the garments of salvation, he hath covered me with the robe of righteousness, as a bridegroom decketh himself with ornaments, and as a bride adorneth herself with her jewels." Isa 61:10

New
Life!

PUT ON THE NEW PERSON

Put on the Lord Jesus Christ
Romans 13:14

A new life means a normal life is starting, a life without corruption, without bribes

"What shall we say then? Are we to continue in sin that grace may abound? By no means! How can we who died to sin still live in it? Do you not know that all of us who have been baptized into Christ Jesus were baptized into his death? We were buried therefore with him by baptism into death, in order that, just as Christ was raised from the dead by the glory of the Father, we too might walk in newness of life. For if we have been united with him in a death like his, we shall certainly be united with him in a resurrection like his. " Rom 6:

This means that anyone who belongs to Christ has become a new person. The old life is gone; a new life has begun!" (2 Cor 5:17 NLT) As a result, we are no longer under the curse of sin and darkness, but are given all the blessings listed in Deuteronomy 28:3-13

Now then, the action of putting on Christ becomes daily nourishment through prayer, worship and reading/studying the Bible. By choosing to spend time in the presence of The Lord, is the same as deciding what clothing to put on before presenting ourselves to the world. "Like newborn babies, you must crave pure spiritual milk so that you will grow into a full experience of salvation. Cry out for this nourishment." 1 Peter 2:2 NLT

Hello
Winter

Winter Wonder

The coldest of the seasons not only from the wind
But betrayal of a family member or friend
This external blow is designed to turn you inwardly
Much like the trunk preserving the life of a tree
Deeper and deeper it flows beneath the earth for its strength
Shedding from it everything hidden hindering it's length
Cheer up this season must come and have its way
In His arms of safety is the best place to lay
I know it's tough right now being naked and exposed
This is the wonder of winter and how the soul grows

Cool & Casual

ARIZONA

Arizona, the Grand Canyon state, was originally part of Spanish and Mexican territories. The land was ceded to the United States in 1848 and became a separate territory in 1863. Arizona officially earned its statehood in 1912

Arizona is the sixth largest state in the country in terms of area. Most of its population lives in urban areas, especially since the mid-20th century. To truly understand Arizona means walking ancient paths. Take time to learn about the first peoples that populated the land as you explore prehistoric dwellings, the weathered remains of entire villages, artwork etched into rocks, relics and artifacts that are all part of the archeological legacy left behind by different cultures.

MATHER POINT

THE GRAND CANYON

National Park

The Grand Canyon is considered one of the natural wonders of the world largely because of its natural features. The exposed geologic strata - layer upon layer from the basement Vishnu schist to the capping Kaibab limestone - rise over a mile above the river, representing one of the most complete records of geological history that can be seen anywhere in the world. Geologic formations such as gneiss and schist found at the bottom of the Canyon date back 1,800 million years. This geologic incline creates a diversity of biotic communities, and five of the seven life zones are present in the park.

The entire park area is considered to be semi-arid desert, but the views are spectacular. The South Rim is the most popular and convenient way to experience the grand canyon since it offers a variety of viewpoints.

SOUTH RIM

FROSTED LAKES

Kaibab & Cataract Campgrounds

Kaibab National Forest offers layers of opportunity for peace, solitude and discovery. Kaibab Lake sits among the diverse landscape of Kaibab National Forest of northern Arizona. The lake is a popular spot for fishing and picnicking, as well as for RV and motorhome campers. With Grand Canyon National Park just 60 miles north and several other cultural and historic sites nearby, the location is a hotspot for recreation, learning and sightseeing. While visiting Williams Arizona, I happen to make a stop at the Kaibab and Cataract lake/campgrounds without any idea of what to expect.

When I got to the parking area I was captivated by the lakes from a distance, but as I got closer I realized the lakes were frozen. Since I grew up in South Florida, a frozen lake is not something you would normally see. But I wasn't alone, there were a few people visiting as well, who you could tell felt the same way. Before you knew it, we were all throwing rocks like kids around the lake's edge while trying to see how far we could go before the ice broke; the fun was so exilerating a star came out to witness. This first time experience was never on my bucket list, but it sure topped it off. GH

Bill Williams Mountain

BILL WILLIAMS MOUNTAIN

Bill Williams Mountain is a high mountain peak at an elevation of 2.822m (9,259ft) above the sea level, located in Coconino County, in the north-central part of the U.S. state of Arizona. It's one of the highest mountain roads of Arizona.

Located south of Williams, within the Kaibab National Forest, which borders both the north and south rims of the Grand Canyon. The road to the summit is totally unpaved - It's called Forest Road 111. The road is well maintained but steep and usually impassable in winters. William Sherley "Old Bill" Williams was a noted mountain man and frontiersman, known as Lone Elk to the Native Americans. Fluent in several languages, William served as an interpreter for the government and led several expeditions to the West.

LAKE HAVASU CITY

ARIZONA'S PLAYGROUND

Lake Havasu City is in western Arizona. It's known as a base for trails in the nearby desert and water sports on Lake Havasu. London Bridge, relocated from England, links the mainland to marinas and a looped path in an area known as the Island. The Lake Havasu Museum of History documents Native American and steamboat history. Lake Havasu State Park has beaches with mountain views, plus picnic spots and birdlife.

Lake Havasu is where adrenaline meets tranquility, a water paradise where fun knows no limits. The wide-open waterways of Lake Havasu and the Lower Colorado River offer breathtaking space for adventures in boating, fishing, and watersports. It provides easy access to the Arizona Peace Trail, a 750-mile-long off-highway vehicle (OHV) loop that offers diverse terrain spanning the most beautiful parts of the southwestern U.S. desserts.

THE LONDON BRIDGE

ABIDING IN THE WORD OF GOD

If ye abide in me, and my words abide in you, ye shall ask what ye will, and it shall be done unto you.
John 15:7

WHY THE WORD OF GOD IS ESSENTIAL TO HEALTH

... incline thine ear unto my sayings. Let them not depart from thine eyes; keep them in the midst of thine heart. For they are life unto those that find them, and health to all their flesh.
Prov. 4:20-22

The Bible is the Authoritative & Inerrant breathed out word of God

The Bible is not only a physical book, it is a supernatural Source of Good. It is God's Living Water (His Presence) moving through our lives (John 7:38) as we read it. Read the Bible and God's energy pours into our lives.

"For the word of God is alive and powerful. It is sharper than the sharpest two-edged sword, cutting between soul and spirit, between joint and marrow. It exposes our innermost thoughts and desires." Hebrews 4:12 (NLT)

Reading the Bible is to the spirit like water is to the body, it purifies! Reading the Bible gets rid of all the spiritual toxins (doubt, worry, fear, etc.) and replaces them with pure liquid Jesus and all that's good found in Him! Reading the Bible refreshes and revives us!

We can live in victory because the Bible is cutting out all that is not of God and replacing it with things that actually help us overcome. Letting God correct us by reading the Bible leaves room for Him to equip us. Reading the Bible gives us everything we need each day to be victorious!

The well-spring of Jesus' healing power is found in the Bible. Once we fully believe God and His promises found in His Word, our faith will activate Jesus' power in our spiritual, physical, relational, emotional and mental lives! We just need to read the Bible to get that power!   CBN

Nutritional Health

A CLOSER LOOK

THE TRUTH ABOUT NUTRITION

Nutritional science is the science that studies the physiological process of nutrition (primarily human nutrition), interpreting the nutrients and other substances in food in relation to maintenance, growth, reproduction, health and disease of an organism.

Modern nutrition science began in the 1910s as individual micronutrients began to be identified. The first vitamin to be chemically identified was thiamine in 1926, and vitamin C was first to be found as a protection against scurvy in 1932. The role of vitamins in nutrition was studied in the following decades. The first recommended dietary allowances for humans were developed in fear of disease caused by food deficiencies around the time of the Great Depression and second world war

The seven major classes of nutrients are carbohydrates, fats, fiber, minerals, proteins, vitamins, and water. Nutrients can be grouped as either macronutrients or micronutrients (needed in small quantities). Carbohydrates, fats, and proteins are macronutrients, and provide energy. Water and fiber are macronutrients but do not provide energy. The micronutrients are minerals and vitamins.

ANTIOXIDANTS

To reap the benefits of antioxidants, reach for a handful of fresh, juicy berries; foods with rich, vibrant colors often contain the most antioxidants. Antioxidants are considered free radical scavengers. Flavonoids, flavones, catechins, polyphenols, and phytoestrogens are all types of antioxidants and phytonutrients, and they are all found in plant-based foods. Exposure to air pollution, heavy metals, and cigarette smoke can cause free radical damage, increasing the risk of autoimmune diseases, diabetes, heart disease, Parkinson's disease, Alzheimer's disease, and cancer.

MEET THE SCIENCE AESTHETICS

Nutritional science was born in the early years of the twentieth century with the then revolutionary recognition that the absence of something could produce disease. It also deals with the organism's responses to the diet. It includes studies not only on the nutrients themselves but also on molecular interactions, metabolic and signaling pathways, physiology, pathology, and toxicology. The biochemical and physiological process by which an organism uses food to support its life is the purpose of nutrition, because it ncludes ingestion, absorption, assimilation, biosynthesis, catabolism and excretion. The concept of metabolism, the transfer of food and oxygen into heat and water in the body, creating energy, was discovered in 1770 by Antoine Lavoisier, the "Father of Nutrition and Chemistry."

Mental Health

THE SURE WAY OF MENTAL HEALTH

Thou will keep him in perfect peace whose Mind is stayed on thee: because he trusteth in thee Isaiah 26:3

According to the World Health Organization, mental health is a state of well-being in which an individual realizes his or her own abilities, can cope with the normal stresses of life, can work productively and is able to make a contribution to his or her community.

Chronic stress has been reported all around the world and is proven to deteriorate the hippocampus; a complex brain structure embedded deep into the temporal lobe which plays a major role in learning and memory.

This stress also leads to decreased concentration and memory, confusion, loss of sense of humor, anger, irritability, and fear. Obviously, stress is not good for the brain, and improved mental health practices can reduce the risk.

However, our psyches, our inner selves, our souls, are hope machines - Our psyches burn hope like our bodies burn energy. And like our bodies grow faint when we run low on energy, when we run low on hope we start feeling discouraged, even desperate. All the wonderful things that have happened to us in the past will not fuel our hope if our future looks bleak. We can be grateful for the past, but we must have hope for the future in order to keep going.

"The human heart is designed to love God most, and is never happier than when it does. The human soul is designed to find its rest in the promises God himself makes to us. The human psyche is designed to find its security in the unconditional acceptance and love of its Creator. And the human body is designed to work best when the heart, soul, and mind are functioning in a harmonious love for and trust in God." - Jon Bloom from Desiring God

Skincare Health

Cozy & Flawless

The ultimate goal of skincare is a clear and perfect tone, free of spots, dark circles under the eyes or blemishes, which is sometimes achieved by washing the face regularly twice a day. This simple routine enhances the skin's natural exfoliation process. However, no matter where you live, the climate or season, we are inevitably exposed to pollutants that can cause skin damage. As a result, maintaining flawless skin during the winter might mean taking a trip by your favorite cosmetic counter for a softening lotion. A hydration lotion not only moisturizes but it revitilizes your skin and should be applied before foundation. As seen here with the model Brittney, a Mac user, has elegantly layered her own makeup and poses a flawless look. She is also wearing her hair down, as opposed to pulled back, to prevent breakage. Her nails are freshly manicured with a soft pastel color to compliment her blinging diamond ring. The grey sweat shirt adds the perfect touch to this cozy moment

Smiling Health

When you smile, your brain releases tiny molecules called neuropeptides to help fight off stress. Then other neurotransmitters like dopamine, serotonin and endorphins come into play too. The endorphins act as a mild pain reliever, whereas the serotonin is an antidepressant. One study even suggests that smiling can help us recover faster from stress and reduce our heart rate. In fact, it might even be worth your while to fake a smile and see where it gets you. There's been some evidence that forcing a smile can still bring you a boost in your mood and happiness level. Stress can permeate our entire being, and it can really show up in our faces. Smiling not only helps to prevent us from looking tired, worn down, and overwhelmed but it can actually help decrease stress. The next time you're feeling down, try putting on a smile, there's a good chance your mood will change for the better.

Fashion for men and women during the winter can be trendy as well as cost effective by wearing a style suitable for daily recreation or evening entertainment (Front Cover). Seen here, Justin is wearing an all black polar collection, including a pair of waterproof gloves and hiking boots.

Physical Health

UNDER CONTROL

BENEFITS OF PHYSICAL HEALTH

WHO defines physical activity as any bodily movement produced by skeletal muscles that requires energy expenditure. Physical activity refers to all movement including during leisure time, for transport to get to and from places, or as part of a person's work. Both moderate- and vigorous-intensity physical activity improve health.

Popular ways to be active include walking, cycling, wheeling, sports, active recreation and play, and can be done at any level of skill and for enjoyment by everybody.

Regular physical activity is proven to help prevent and manage noncommunicable diseases such as heart disease, stroke, diabetes and several cancers. It also helps prevent hypertension, maintain healthy body weight and can improve mental health, quality of life and well-being.

FULL BODY FITNESS

Incorporating flexibility into your day could equate to improved fitness for everyday activities and enhanced overall health and well-being. Stretching can increase flexibility and improve your joints' range of motion by helping you move more freely. What's more, ensuring that you have equal flexibility on both sides might help protect you from injury. Hold a stretch for about 30 seconds, to the point of a slight pull, on each side. Repeat the stretch on both sides 2 to 4 times at least 2 to 3 days a week.

MAKING A MILD IMPACT

Adding dumbbell weights to your workout routine is an excellent way to boost the amount of calories you burn, increase your muscle tone, promote bone density, and ramp up your metabolism. Even if you don't want to bulk up, everyone should aim to increase the density of their muscle mass. The benefits include: burning more calories at rest (even when you're not exercising), more efficient blood flow, increasing support for joints, the ability to perform more challenging body movements, increased stamina and energy, for women, less painful menstrual cycles, managing chronic conditions like back pain, diabetes, obesity, and heart disease, preventing osteoporosis, since stressing your bones leads to an increase in bone density. Strength training is vital to overall health and fitness for everyone, regardless of age.

The
Wedding
Day

To My Son Justin

Though others didn't see me
I was right there by your side
As you looked down the aisle
Toward your beautiful new bride
I heard all of your vows
That both of you said
Standing there with you
Listening with tears as you read
I saw your first dance as a husband
I watched from an empty chair
While smiling from ear to ear
Only wishing I could be there
I couldn't imagine your special day
Without me being a part
Because I'm the one who loved you first
Right from the very start!

I Love You, Mom

Justin & Brittney Are Now Married

They married 25, February 2023 on a beautiful day in South Florida before the company of well wishers, family and friends. This was the big day for my son, and due to circumstances beyond my control, I did not attend the wedding; one of the worst seasons of my life. Still, it's hard to believe that more than 30 years ago he was announced by the doctor, who danced to music that played in the background as he cut the cord. I had been in labor just hours before, after having laughed the entire time before reaching the hospital; probably because I'd already decided to name him Justin, which means humorous, just, upright and stunningly handsome. I can't help thinking about the little boy fully dressed as a cowboy, right down to the genuine leather chaps that always made our rottweiler Sausha bark, I guess she thought you had a horse too. I'm so proud to see how you've grown into a responsible young man, a loving husband and father to be. I stillI remember our conversation about your decision to get married to the woman you now call wifey. I recall how you couldn't believe it was such a treasure in finding her. A few months later I received the photos which are featured on the front cover and throughout this issue of the day you proposed. Thank you for including me in the process of your special day. Congratulations again on your wedding! Mr & Mrs Justin T Humphrey. May the blessings of God rest on your marriage!

Love, Your Proud Mom!

Justice

Poetic Devotion

Injustice cannot be exposed
Without the light of conscious to impose
There comes a time when you have to make a choice
Give up your seat or give up your voice
No backing down - afraid to make a fuss
Make a stand- seated or under the bus
Love and Justice will find a way
Where silence can no longer stay
We have come this far by worse
Surely the last shall be first

ALSO AVAILABLE

The Poetic Devotion Collection

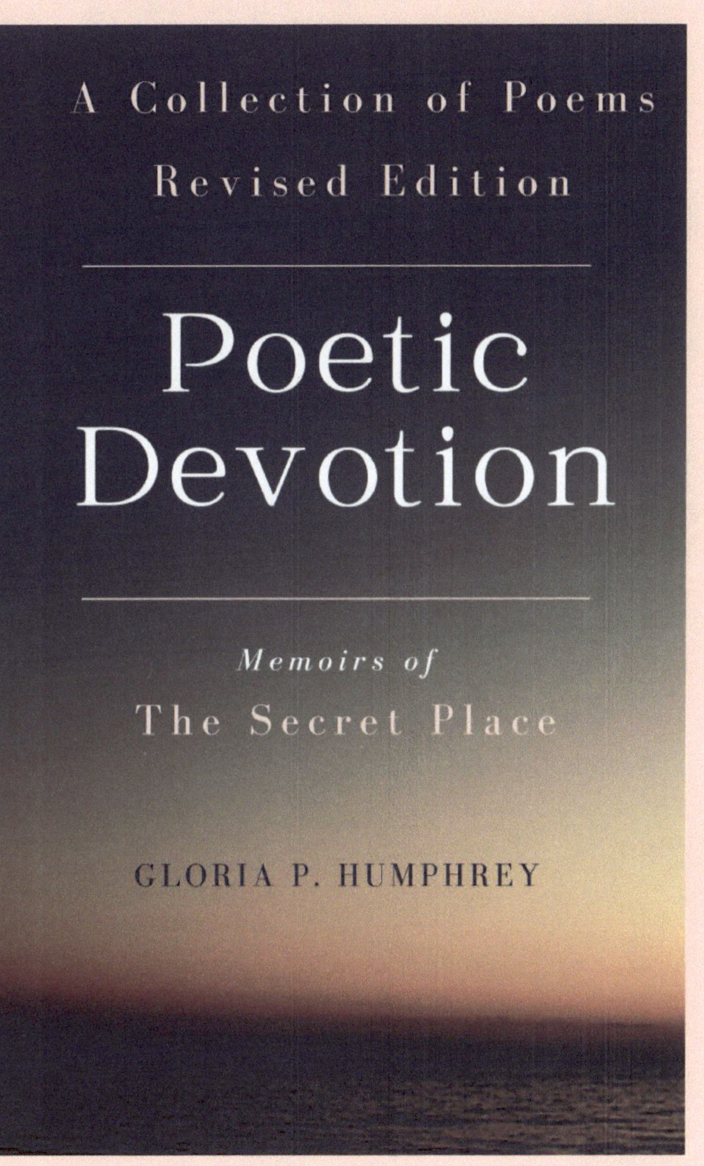

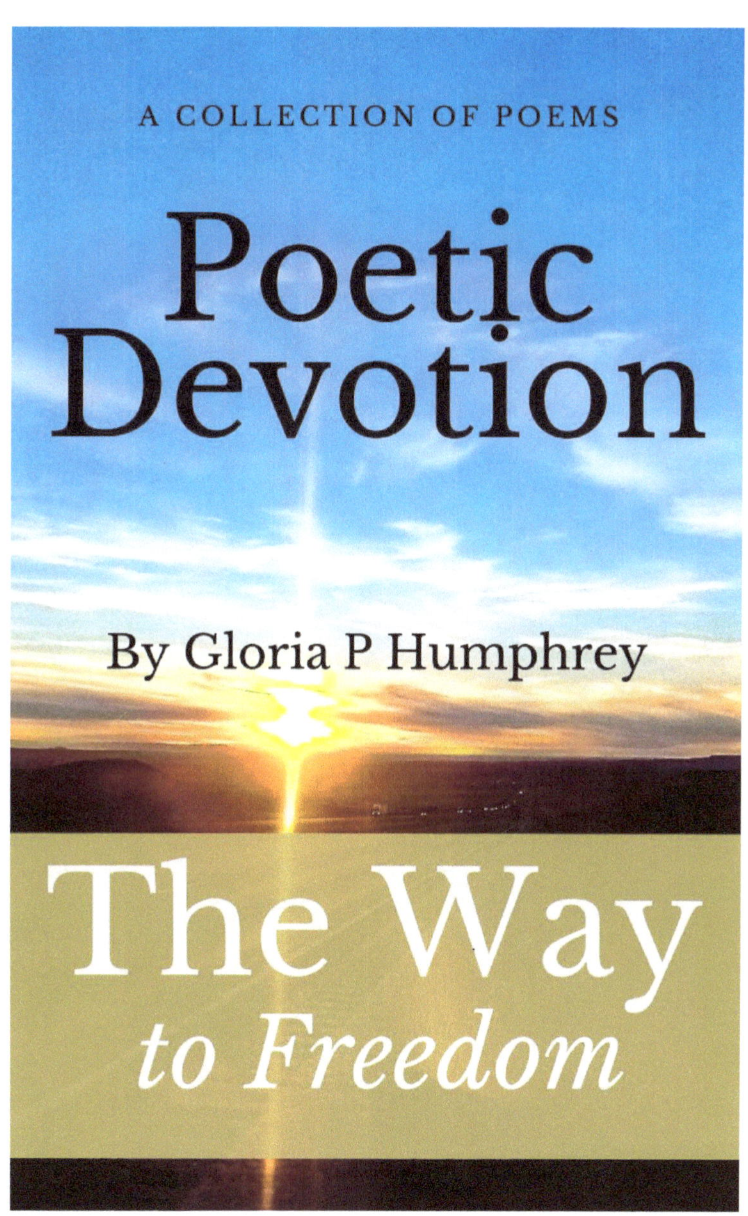

ALSO AVAILABLE

STREET PHOTOGRAPHY

VOLUME NO. 1   THE BLACK & WHITE ISSUE $15.00

FEATURING: **Over 75 Life Size Photos**